Quit

Or Embrace your job Crisis

Mathy Lisika-Minsende

http://whathejobisthis.com
http://about.me/MathyLisikaMinsende

CONTENT

Thank you

I dedicate this book in loving memory of my mother and father. Josephine and Lemy Simon Lisika. Today I live for you, forever I live for you.

To my friends who've supported me both present and past. You may not be here today but I thank you for always believing in me. You are always in my heart.

Victoria Olubi, Jacqui Shaw, thank you for your advice and being on my case in the completion of this book.

INTRODUCT ION

Where it all started.....

I would love to tell you a beautiful story of how I found the job and career of my dreams with the stroke of a magic wand and "poof, there it is!" Except, that's not quiet how it happened -- If it was, it would be one of those stories in which my degree would have seen me overcome all obstacles. It's also the one in which I would be handsomely compensated with a generous redundancy lump sum.

The truth is none of the above applies to me. I don't own a degree. The only thing I got from my last job was a salary. I was too comfortable and later too scared to quit my job. Does that sound like you? I never even quit my last job, it was the loss of my dad and job that gave me the courage to quit the 9-5 and start a business. Nevertheless, I'm grateful that I had to lose what matters most for me to understand when it is time to Quit or embrace your job crisis. I actually think it's great that my story doesn't sound like everyone else's makes it more interesting and easy to relate. My journey has been an extremely trying one, but nonetheless a happy one.

On my excuses

I've been trying to write a book since 2005. My mum knew about it, my dad will never get to see it but **you** will. You are a very, very lucky person and I'm soooo jealous of you right now. I shouldn't be, but I am. This probably doesn't make any sense to you but as you read, listen, or watch my story unfold online you'll know why. I will be making a lot of references to my parents throughout this book; please be patient with me, they are a huge source of encouragement for me and I hope they will be for you too.

The reasons you are reading this book.........

Let's face it; you're too scared of quitting your job! You really don't know how to? I mean, what is the first step? You're bored of this mundane living? You, need an easy way out, that way, you don't look like a fool in front of your peers, your family and colleagues. What type of signs should you look out for? Do you need a plan? What other viable options are out there, for you to walk away, with some form of dignity and faith in yourself.

If you dig deep, you'll probably find that what you need is

an honest, personal self-talk. No more lying to that person in the mirror. This time it's not just about what your friends will say, it's personal. That's why you are reading.

So how personal is it?

Are you anxious, stressed, depressed and damn unhappy with your current job or career? Are you seeking a new **direction for your JOB or career?** Are you looking for fulfilment at work or need to add more **meaning in life? Maybe discover how you can make a difference to the world**? Even find **purpos**e in what you do? Are you getting somewhere, or perhaps you feel that you are getting nowhere? Do you feel that you are drowning, drowning, so much so that you try to stay afloat and becomes numb with

the favourite drug of your choice? Your **JOB.**

READER BEWARE

Just to make you aware, I am neither a psychologist nor qualified councillor. The advice I'm giving is purely based on experience and techniques I have used in the last 14 years, working with thousands of people, helping them find happy jobs and careers. So if you don't resonate with something written in this book, please use common sense .

THIS IS WHAT YOU WILL LEARN – **the importance of living** a more fulfilled life. Knowing when to quit, or stay on a job. Understanding the serious consequences of not living a more balanced and fulfilled life. Listening to your intuition. Avoiding ill-health and depression caused by stress, horrible work cultures and environments. Knowing your values and strengths. Taking control of your career choice. Reinventing you. Rebuilding your confidence from scratch after being used to working in a difficult environment. Experiencing post-traumatic stress disorder (PTSD) due to work. Quitting a job responsibly. Attracting the right employers who share your values. If you like what you've read so far, then keep reading!

"Because work should always be a true reflection of who you are"

CHAPTER ONE

The "*Whathejobisthis*"moment?
"If you don't like something, change it. If you can't change it, change your attitude."

Maya Angelou

Most people don't just up and quit their job for me it was a series of event. It was 5 years, being stuck in a rut and procrastinating, before I first experienced my "Whathejobisthis?" moment.

A **Whathejobisthis** moment **(WTJIT)**; a moment of awakening that stirs you to embrace your calling and do the thing you were called to do in life.

In other words it's your crossroads in life.

In my **"*Whathejobisthis?*"** moment, I realised:

- My job is good only when it is at the initial stage.
- My job is good when I'm learning something from it.
- My job is good when I don't prioritize it over people, family, health, and myself.
- My job is good when it completely fulfils me, my calling and makes me happy.

My job is not good when it's a façade of what truly makes me happy.
My job is not good when it takes over my social and personal life.
My job is not good when it stifles my creativity.
My job is not good when I am getting bullied at work.
My job is not good when I am no longer learning and feel stuck in a rut.
My job is not good when my sister is sick and I'm too stressed to visit her.
My job is not good when my mother is dying and I don't

know if spending time with her is a priority.

Not only is it not good, it also has a long-term impact on your health and well-being.

I remember a time when I used to get up every morning on time, have a shower, breakfast and then crumble at the edge of my bed, crying. I didn't understand why I was crying, but after 20 to 30 minutes of heavy sobbing, I was ready to go and start my day at work.

And this is when I knew I needed an exit-plan and a strategy to escape.

WHAT IS YOUR REASON FOR CHANGE?

" When the student is ready, the teacher will appear"

I always thought financial freedom was a strong enough reason for me to quit my unhappy job and live on a beach. Yep, making more money, getting what I deserved and rightfully owed to me. I was dabbling in direct sales, network marketing business, property ownership and all sorts of graft and hustle. It had to be done because I was determined to work towards a prosperous future. I also thought time was on my side and felt that I could skip the research and get onto the fast track. I guess I had the wrong reasons, took the wrong paths, and that's why it took me almost 9 years to write a book. I complained, procrastinated, didn't persevere long enough in my business ventures and kept feeling cheated, depressed and disappointed until bitterness overwhelmed me.

It wasn't until experiences with loss and death when I realised how important life is. I was always grateful for what I have, and for the most part, a positive and motivated person. However I admit that discouragement and depression were lurking round the corner. At my mum's funeral in March 2008, I started taking more responsibility in life. By the time we had to cope with my dad's funeral in March 2011, I was a different person.

All in the span of three years like a part in a horror movie. It was as if a piece of me had been buried in that coffin that day I lost my dad. With no job, no mum, no dad and no more savings, there was nothing left of me. Whilst I felt vulnerable, I also felt a pressing sense of urgency not to go to my grave without leaving something to be remembered by.

I remember these words from the various strangers at different times of my life: "Your mum and dad were such generous and helpful people; you'll always be blessed wherever you go", "Your dad helped me with my school fees", "Oh wow, I didn't realise he was your dad; he kept me off the streets and out of trouble so many times", "Your mum was like a second mum to me". It was beautiful, scary, upsetting and a lot of pressure.

And that's when the impetus for change began to surface. I wanted to have that kind of impact and influence on people; the kind where they'd never forget the positive effects I had on them. This was my reason; my impetus for change. I wanted to leave a legacy and die with no regrets because death is real and life is honestly too short.

Finding your reason for change

This is what I've learned from this chapter in my life. If you're going to make a decision and choose a reason it's probably motivated by a burning sensation, a frustrating moment and a feeling of life hanging by a thread.

Most clients I've worked with couldn't decide or wouldn't decide. They were just too scared to quit by walking out on their jobs. It was a gradual process that pushed them to jump.

Therefore I have to ask you before you turn this page: do you have a strong-enough reason to quit your job and are you ready to reinvent yourself?

Follow the food for thought on the next page.

Food for Thought...

Which of these wishes apply to you the most?

To be remembered in the hearts of men
To make a difference in other people's lives
To be in full control and in charge of your destiny
To do something more meaningful.
To build a future for your family
To be completely happy
To live stress-free, more healthily and for longer
You have very little time because of a life-threatening illness
You want to check something off the bucket list

If it's something else, please write it underneath

_____

_____

_____

____

_____

CHAPTER TWO

The Signs

"Our intuition is like a ringing alarm clock, ringing relentlessly, but we keep hitting the snooze button and hoping to squeeze in 5 more minutes of sleep"

Mathy Lisika-Minsende

Your intuition

T he alarm rings, it's 7 a.m., I hit the snooze button. It rings again, this time I'm up, turn the music on, jump out of bed, get in the shower, brush my teeth, get dressed, pick up my keys and I'm all ready to go. When all of a sudden, I rush back in to the house to get my phone. I can hear it ringing but I can't see it. "Where is that damn phone?!" I pick it up from the dressing table and the alarm rings again. I wake up and scream, "Oh no, I'm late for work!" I'm still in my pyjamas.

The above story actually happened to me. I hope I'm not the only one facing this scenario. It would be pretty sad, I know. Intuition is an amazing tool which most of us lack the ability to use correctly. Strangely enough, every time when I was caught in an unpleasant situation i.e. relationship, friendship, wrong job or about to be scammed, deep inside, I always knew it was happening. Although the negative outcome is a rude shock, the feeling wasn't. I just kept hitting the snooze button on the alarm clock and avoided having to face the reality for as long as I could because I didn't think the information my subconscious brain sending me was relevant at the time.

Intuition- How to read the signs

Your intuition talks to you all day long but can you hear it? Some people say they never hear it. Well, maybe it's because the music is too loud, literally. For some others, there may be way too many distractions around to prevent them from hearing their intuitions talk. Take the following distractions: other people's opinions, being overworked, technology, lack or rest, unhealthy patterns of stress, personal addiction or addictive behaviour and no time for what should have been Number 1 on the list - YOU!

Of course, there are people who are more intuitive than others (I know I am one of them). But intuition is in-built and everyone can learn to tap into their intuitions. I recommend trying the following steps?

Listening to your intuition:

1. Find a spot where you can be alone and **BE QUIET** (digest any recent information, activities, feelings, situations).
2. Turn off all communication devices, switch off every digital platform.
3. Observe patterns in yourself, in people, situations and your surroundings.
4. Be aware of that tight knot in your stomach and listen to that still, small voice.
5. Keep a diary - written/audio/video.
6. Become more aware of patterns which make you happy or unhappy.

IT'S TIME - DO SOMETHING!

The Alarm, The Plan, The Preparation

You've heard of the fight or flight response; when the nervous system sends signals that you may be in some kind of threat or danger, and then your brain and body begin to prepare you to "fight" or "flee".

Once upon a time we faced real dangers in the form of **sabre-toothed tigers**. Imagine walking around London, Trafalgar Square to be precise, at 3 p.m. in the afternoon, on a hot, sunny day. All of a sudden, you come face to face with a real life sabre-toothed tiger (not the Madame Tussaud- style ones, please). Any other person would run or freeze, but Londoners would probably take out their phones, take a picture, post it on their YouTube, Facebook and after a couple of hundred thousand views later, be screened on TV. Dude! You' are already dead by now!

Come on, you should be running. If anything, all of your senses should have intensified -- pupils dilating, you become more aware of your surroundings and are physically and psychologically more prepared for fight or flight.

Whilst we may not be facing any attacks from real **sabre-toothed tigers,** but there are still real life situations that can be as threatening as attacks from **sabre-toothed tigers.**

No matter how real or unreal these physical threats might appear to be, the release of toxic chemicals produced and pumped through your body every day is not good for anyone's long term health.

Below, you'll find real examples of threats which might be an indication that you are in some form of *"attacked by a sabre-toothed tiger"* situation and if you can relate to these examples, it may be time to do something about it. The bottom line is this: if you value yourself, then you value your health.

The abusive work relationship and horrible bosses-the obvious sign.

You on a Monday Morning

You come in to the office as early as you can to get work done, get some peace and quiet and set the right tone for the rest of the work week. Work is so pleasant when it just involves you and your colleagues. But you know you only have 45 minutes before Godzilla stomps into the building. You hope that she'll forget about the meeting today. You imagine that one of her kids will be ill or in hospital, or her husband is involved in a car crash (with no one dying or any serious injuries, of course).

You just hope for something drastic to have happened to keep you off her radar. Hopefully she won't notice what you're wearing today and make a horrible comment about your hair, your weight, or send you home because you are wearing the wrong shoes, or make you stay behind a few extra hours when she knows you have your best friend's birthday drinks to attend tonight. You're hoping you'll have the guts to tell her to stop humiliating you or yelling at you in meetings.

You knew the first time she smiled at you; it was really just a smirk. And when she complimented you on your hair, she really hated it and was simply being sarcastic. The way she would talk to other colleagues in your presence and then stare at you and laugh. The way she would include you in meetings to mine ideas but never acknowledge your opinions.

At reviews, when you suggest a course for your CPD (Continuing Personal Development), she would suggest something of a mediocre or lower standard than what you were clearly capable of. You cringe whenever you see her. When she looks at you, you see disgust written all over her face. You step out of the way when she walks towards you; not out of respect, but because you wanted to get out of her path of destruction in case you get hurt.

Every time she calls your name you have palpitations in your chest and sweaty palms, or forget what you were about to say. You cry on the way to work, in the office toilet, you cry on the way home. You have a horrible boss and deep inside you know that you'll never grow or progress in the company, if you stay where you are and say nothing.

"People who value themselves, value their health."

Pay attention to the gradual and subtle signs -

<u>Me on Tuesday Morning</u>

Unhappy at work was not my SOP (Standard Operating Procedure). If anything, *happy* was my nickname. Everyone at work knew I was **Happy Mathy**, but I gradually started to feel unchallenged. I kept feeling that there was more to me than delivering marketing sales presentations. I wanted to motivate others, write and speak to crowds because this is something that made me happy all the time. I started feeling the urge to jump ship. I felt curious about life beyond this professional façade and, the need for excitement. And I did that several times. But after the initial exhilaration of having jumped ship, I was unhappy again -- I needed the freedom to express my creativity. I started realising that I was denying myself the truth; denying myself the fulfilment of utmost satisfaction.

<u>By Wednesday Morning</u>

Distracted and Bored - "I AAAAAAAAAAAAAM bored!" Outgrowing my role, finishing all my assignments quickly, spending more time on the Internet reading blogs. Then....

<u>Me on Thursday Morning</u>

Procrastinating - Complaining about things that make me unhappy:
- My computer screen
- My office
- This year's Christmas party
- Handing my work in late
- Turning late for work

Every excuse you can think of.

<u>Me on Friday Morning</u>

Depressed - loss of purpose and motivation.
This morning I cried so often I couldn't keep count. Before I got dressed, in the shower, whilst having breakfast -- I think it was more like Kellogg's' *Tears*-Flakes. Now I don't know where I am, there are people around me but I feel like I'm drowning again and again in a sea of moving

people and they can't see me. My mouth is open but no words come out. Across the road I can see my office but I can't see any of the cars. I get inside the office and happiness has completely left me. I have a still, emotionless, ghost-like face.

"People who value themselves, value their health."

Like being involved in any other type of abusive relationship, you don't realise it's time to go, you allow your brain to get used to those abusive habits, you are desensitized and accept them to be normal. This later causes post-traumatic stress. Then, when you eventually leave that job, utterly spent, you wonder what went wrong.

Happy choice - Happy work life
Why it matters to be happy at work:

- The average person spends almost 90,000 hours at work in a lifetime.
- For the benefit of health in the long run.
- For personal growth and development.
- To make a genuine difference on this planet with the use of your skills and ability.
- To gives a sense of belonging and identity.
- When you are happy at work you are more positive, enabling you to contribute constructively in other areas of your life as well.
- Reduce break-ups in relationships and family.
- Because it makes you feel valued and that you matter.

- For a sense of accomplishment that every person needs.
- If you're going to do something, you might as well do it well and complete it now.

If you're not happy at work, or you're not exactly skipping down the road and looking forward it, do something! Don't be an eternal sour-puss. You won't attract the right career that way. It's time to make a change.

If you look at it in another way, work is almost like a marriage, so it'd be wise to choose carefully if you intend to spend the equivalent of half a lifetime, or even if you are planning to spend a shorter amount of time with it. Don't be fooled by a short-term status - know what you're getting into. We all hope for a "happily-ever-after relationship" outcome in personal relationships, so why should work be any different? Why suffer in silence at an unhappy workplace where you feel unvalued and demotivated?

Make sure that you: "**Own your resistance**". I talk about it in my video on

Resistance Are you resisting yourself Watch my video on Resistance

REFLECTION

When is it too late?

"It is easier to live in our virtual reality than. Rise to the challenge, taking the plunge and changing direction in life."

Mathy Lisika-Minsende

F or me, being out of work was okay; being unemployed however, was never an option. Was I lazy? Yes sometimes, if not properly motivated but I always need to have something productive to do. I always knew what I wanted and who I was. This was a quality that was required in my field of work. As an employment specialist, I was everyone's best friend, I had an answer for pretty much everything; a tip for every day of the week and a solution for every problem. But on March 25th 2011, at 4 a.m., my life quickly became meaningless. I ran out of gas when a phone call from Paris awakened me abruptly. I got that sinking feeling in my stomach and knew it would be bad; it was always bad news if it was delivered at that time. In my heart of hearts I knew it was coming. My father had a 3-year battle with cancer, but I was always hopeful that that he would overcome all odds and survive. But at 4 a.m. that morning, he had lost the battle. The caller was my sister, announcing that dad had passed away. I would have to travel to Paris for the burial and mourning period.

I was painfully aware of the imminent job cuts at the company I worked at, announced 4 months earlier. My extended absence meant that I had served myself on the chopping board and would be axed. For the first time in my life, I was truly indecisive. On hindsight, I was just using my dad's cancer and my career dilemma to avoid taking any action. They were my security blankets and I hid under them. It would take another 6 to 10 months for me before I was on the road to recovery.

If you don't learn the first time, then life will keep giving you the same scenarios in a different package and you will have to learn again and again and again until you get it.

Watch my video on Being Grateful! On being grateful

CHAPTER THREE

<u>Dig deep</u>

"It is not your CV or experience that stops you from moving forward in your career, it's your mind-set. The way you communicate with yourself blocks any opportunity to attract the right career."

Mathy Lisika-Minsende

When the root of the problem isn't clear anymore

It's time to dig deep
So far, this is what we've been taught by various institutions: Happiness at work is a simple formula. This is at the **surface level**. Here's the equation: **Schooling + Education + Good Job = Lifelong security**

My 'iceberg theory' in a different context (it has nothing to do with Ernest Hemingway's.)

An iceberg is not just another little block of ice floating along in the ocean. If you came across one, you would know that only one eighth of it is visible above the water line. Some are the size of a car and others are a little bit bigger than Wales in the UK. Be careful - this usually means that what lies beneath the surface is more alarming.

The depths of your career happiness at lies in the choice you make today just like an ICEBERG. Life may sometimes look like a straightforward computer program, it's not and neither is it a 'bug-free' one. Ultimately, we are not machines but human beings - flesh and blood with real needs and emotions. So stop treating yourself like computer hardware (and think you can push yourself like a machine) and expect life to run smoothly like a 'bug-free' computer program.

Before focusing on your CV or any surface strategy,

work firstly on the root of the matter.

A lady by the name of Janet came to see me for a coaching session. She was a married mum of a little girl and had previously worked in retail banking. She was on maternity leave but was quite anxious about going back to work. And although all she asked me for was to update her CV, I quickly realised that was not what she really wanted. Underneath the surface, this is what was happening:

- She was in an unhappy marriage, one in which her husband was controlling and manipulative;
- She had lost her self-esteem and identity;
- She really disliked retail banking;
- She wanted to engage people and teach.

But she felt paralysed and didn't know how to approach the situation.

It's not until she opened up about her 'iceberg situation' that we were able to break away from the obstacles she was facing. She has dealt successfully with her 'iceberg' and now works as a trainer in adult education.

"The quality of your life is the quality of your personal communication "
Anthony Robbins

The way in which you communicate with yourself will have a serious impact on your happiness at work and the results you get.

HERE IS MY INTERPREPRETATION OF ANTHONY ROBBINS' QUOTE:

If you say; **I'm lucky I even have a job** (what you also mean) **= I have no control over my career choice**

Time to change the patterns

So if this is what we have been taught since childhood:

Schooling + Education + Good job = Lifelong security.

We need to change that equation a little and replace some out-of-date information with what's really happening.

Education + Experience + Communicating with Yourself + Healthy Relationships + Choosing Yourself + Changing Your Mindset + Adapting to New Problems + Rebranding Your Marketability= Security for life

It's your turn now - start a new formula:

$$\frac{\underline{\hspace{3cm}} + \underline{\hspace{3cm}}}{\underline{\hspace{2cm}} + \underline{\hspace{2cm}}} + \underline{\hspace{2cm}} = \textbf{Security for life}$$

CHAPTER FOUR

The healing process

"Loss is a gift, not a curse, the quicker you accept the train ticket, the lighter the ride."

Mathy Lisika-Minsende

P eople naturally stay away from thoughts or feelings of losing someone close to them. The pain of reliving memories of what will no longer be, and the acceptance of having to say goodbye signify too great a defeat. You go through the same negative feelings when experiencing the loss of a job. Having these feelings is a natural part of the grieving. If you were to have your left arm cut off because of an accident or a medical condition, you would mourn it too. But, after getting past the grief, what can you learn from the loss?

When you experience loss or redundancy, you may not realise it now but taking time out, is good for you. It's like a car that needs to have its MOT check.

There are 5 stages of **Loss** also known as the **Change Curve of Grief**.

DENIAL
ANGER
BARGAINING
DEPRESSION
ACCEPTANCE

1st - We are shocked at the news and deny that it's happening

2nd - We are then angry at everyone, including ourselves

3rd - In our helplessness, **we bargain** with anyone and everyone for help

4th - We then lose hope and spiral into **depression**

5th - And finally, **we accept** our path

It's time for you to heal.

Which stages of **Loss** are you at? Where would you like to be?

_____

_____

_____

"Loss is like a seed being planted into the ground; for it to grow and flourish into a beautiful flower, it first needs to die." *Mathy Lisika-Minsende*

How to quit your job? Knowing when it's right

Quitting can be instantaneous, strategic and gradual - the choice is yours.

Instantaneous - Walking out

Strategic - Planning your exit

Gradual - Multi- tasking: building a new career whilst still at the other

What some people believe quitting should be all about:
- Having enough money to **walk out** the door and live comfortably for a little while.
- **Telling the boss what you feel** and making your way into the sunset.
- Having a **job secured before** you make any attempt to **jump ship.**

The truth is there is no right or wrong way to quit. The first part of quitting should, however, start in your mind. The choice is yours and it's down to you to decide what to do. You are in charge of the quitting and hiring and will have to live with the consequences of your actions.

You need to be **responsible** for whatever happens to you. And if nothing happens as you planned, what are you going to do about it? Avoid finding new ways to blame others for your misfortune.

Watch my video on How to quit your job here
Part 1 How to quit Part 1 **and** 2 How to quit Part 2

Here are your steps on how to quit:

- Start with your **REASON for change**. Why are you leaving? Are you unhappy, bored, upset at work, not growing?
- Find out what it is. Acknowledge it, accept it and take action.
- Listen to your intuition (you now know how intuition works, if not, go to chapter 3).
- Don't take the negative comments from others too hard (they mean well, but it's your opinion that counts).
- Expect the unexpected - prepare your mind.
- Take ownership and responsibility for your own actions.
- You have options - get your thinking cap on. **I can quit now**, **get another job** before I quit, or accumulate some **savings, then quit**, or anything else is possible...................

Now that you know the stages of the **Change Curve**, and how to quit, it may be time to **face your villain** and be your own superhero because rescuing starts from within. You owe it to yourself, so start now. Why continue to live a mediocre, unfulfilled life and keep failing at work with something you no longer enjoy, when you can learn to get back up and learn from something worthwhile?

Whatever the decision you make, you are right because whatever happens, you will be able to handle it.

Be your own **superhero!** Most people want someone to

rescue them but you need to rescue yourself.

CHAPTER FIVE

<u>Choosing your career, starts with you</u>

"When I'm willing to share my passion, people are willing to receive me and serve my calling."

Mathy Lisika-Minsende

Acknowledge, Accept, Take action.

It's all about the relationship you choose

Imagine choosing marriage partner for life. Since a marriage is for life, it's quite an important and serious decision; you wouldn't choose a partner because you are desperate no matter how old you are, or because you don't want to be left on the shelf. Well, your workplace is similar to being in a form of committed relationship. You can be committed, casual, a cheater or a partner who is not looking for permanent relationship arrangement. The choice is yours but you have to do it because you will have to live with the choice you have made and not with the comments or decisions of others.

I was 19 and unemployed when I first chose myself. I was having some quiet time, writing in my diary, in shared accommodation for young women -- in Kennington. One Wednesday morning, I started asking myself questions; what I could do to make a difference to this world. The answer I got was this:

"Be an agent of change no matter what you do or where you are".

This is what I did to find out. I drew a table with pluses (+) in one column and minuses (-) in the next. I wrote all the things I liked in the plus column and the things I didn't like in the other column. Just like the table below, it looked something like this:

What can I do to make a difference?

+	-

When you choose yourself, you are **NUMBER 1.** Your decision is not made out of desperation. Here's what we say and what we mean:

- Oh I need this job, it's all I have. ➡️ I depend on this job.
- If I quit, I wouldn't know where to start all over again. ➡️ This job is my sole identity.
- You don't understand; I need to pay my bills. ➡️ This is the only way I know how to make money and my sense of security depends on it.

Honestly, you probably haven't tried anything new or outside your comfort zone because it's scary. Well now is the time to step out of that comfort zone. .
Acknowledge your excuses. Accept the reality and take some action.

So what's your excuse for not making a difference in your work life?

Here's your chance to do some soul searching. What messages do you tell your brain based on the knowledge, pain and experience that prevent you from choosing

NUMBER 1? Write down what you say as a convenient excuse and next to it, what you really mean.

_____

_____

_____

_____

_____

_____

_____

_____

Remember, just like wanting a happy, committed relationship use this time to attract the right career by working on YOURSELF. You really owe it to you.

CHAPTER SIX

Reinvent You!

"Because work should always be a true reflection of who you are"

Mathy Lisika-Minsende

Attracting the right career and opportunity of your dreams starts by reinventing you.

I sometimes give people the impression that I'm living a glamorous life. I'm far from rich! I'm very charismatic. I've learned to magnify that strength over the years. I'm only living a happy life because I step out of my comfort zone regularly. I reinvent myself time and time again. I take calculated risks and I make choices I can live with. Some people ask me; "Hey Mathy, how did you get that for free! How did you land that career? Oh my God, how did you land that opportunity?" They might even say" Mathy, you are so lucky." Luck to me, is a series of action I've been taking over the years, leading me to my opportunity. It's really simple, "my heart is open and my spirit is ready to receive the unexpected. What I cannot conceive". That is my only secret to finding new opportunities and attracting the right people to work with me.

The 3 Ps formula - the 3 important ingredients for you to attract the right career opportunities begin with:

1. **Positive People**
2. **Positive Lifestyle**
3. **Positive Mindset**

Positive People - add new people of various backgrounds to your life, discover new environments, places you've never been before, model the behaviour of highly successful people, have those same people as your mentors, surround yourself with them at any occasion and offer to help them and anyone you come across.

Positive Lifestyle - develop a healthy pattern of living; build a healthy relationship between your body, diet, physical fitness and spiritual well-being. Be easy and gentle on yourself all of the time.

Positive Mindset - educate yourself continuously, reframe your thinking daily, feed your mind the right food, build mental stamina, listen to your intuition, be open-minded, treat every experience as a new opportunity and treat every day as if it were your last.

What will you do today to improve your 3 Ps formula? Fill in the blanks on what you need to do to improve those three areas.

Positive People	Positive Lifestyle	Positive Mindset

12 steps to attracting the right career

Be curious and hungry for change.

Look outside for inward inspiration.

Reinvent yourself; give yourself a makeover, mentally and physically.

Look for people on similar journeys.

Pace yourself, be gentle on you, don't over-do it or get burnt out quickly.

Challenge yourself to learn a new skill or improve an existing one.

Immerse yourself in a new environment.

Apply your new-found skill and put it in to practice.

Create a support network of allies, collaborators and mentors.

Learn to be resourceful with very limited tools and money. Money is never a barrier.

When faced with a difficult situation, prepare your mind for every possible scenario.

Follow a daily podcast, audio or video content that inspires you.

Reassess your value, recycle and repackage.

<u>You are who you've always been.</u>

*"Mathy! Are you still doing the Oprah Winfrey Show again!?"#**French accent***
Mama Lisika

This is a phrase my mum would continuously say to me till I was 25. She would frequently catch me in my room playing with my teddy bears. Aged 11-15, I would stand in front of the mirror with a brush in my hand, talking in front of an audience of 4… teddy bears. That is where the phrase comes from.

I've always lived on purpose.

I have never understood why others don't. Don't worry, I was a weird child, this only happens to me. I'm still weird but that is a different story. I think you're alright. I never had any problem knowing what I was supposed to do in life. So why do so many healthy working adults suffer from exhaustion, stress, escapism and perpetual sense of being lost? Sometimes being a grown-up really isn't as rosy as it's made out to be. You get so caught up in the mundane, you forget what matters most. But little children don't. They see the little details, they pay attention, and they notice things that adults overlook. So maybe there is something to be learned from a child's perspective that you can apply to your current life. Perhaps I could say that there is no such thing as a reinvention? There's nothing on the planet that hasn't already been created, just **Reassessed, Recycled and Repackaged.**

Consider all your options- transferable skills and personal resources.

When my clients tell me:

I don't know what I'm supposed to do, I don't have a purpose in life, I don't have any skills, I ask them what did you like doing as a child? What do you do in your free time? What are your interests? What do people know you for? I've observed various clients, people and family members and noticed that your calling, purpose, ambition and any work-related choice that you make is always closely linked with your childhood experience. The only way to know who you are is by letting the little child roam free. No restrictions. GO!!!!!!!

Children have no restrictions, no boundaries, which is why they have more faith and courage compared to adults. Have you heard the expression 'to have childlike faith'? **Let the little child within find the superhero in you.** If you wouldn't tell your child or niece that they are rubbish at something, then it's time to stop telling yourself that. The beginning of your reinvention starts on the inside and the formula is: **Reassessed, Recycled + Repackaged.** So will you rise to the challenge and try it? Now it's your turn to **reinvent yourself**, starting with you.

"Because work should always be a true reflection of who you are"

Choosing Your career starts by choosing yourself . **The solution is starring you in the face-Transferable skills**

I knew a very creative woman who loved weddings. When you walked into her little flat in Dulwich, where she lived with her 4 children and her husband, all you could see were colourful decorations, flowers, balloons, ribbons and ornaments from previous weddings she had been decorating. She loved weddings so much that decorating weddings became a separate entity, demanding her attention and consuming her time as she cared for them. It was as if she were caring for another member in the house. So when she told me that she wanted to start a wedding planning business I was over the moon for her. But all she could say to me was, "But I don't have the qualifications, nor the experience." I was shocked and surprised at those words because to me, the answer was staring her right in the face. Once, I asked her how long she had been doing weddings. She said, "I've been volunteering at my local church for 17 years". Her day job had nothing to do with weddings, in fact she was a phlebotomist at a children's hospital. I remember challenging her to introduce herself to others as a free-lance wedding planner, create a portfolio of her work, and ask people for feedback. I even assisted as part of her help team at the beginning of the challenge. This was back in 2007. She has now moved to Luton where she is very happy, runs her part time business alongside her part time job and has a garage full of decorations. Something she never imagined that she would be doing today.

I know that a lot of my creative clients never feel as though their art can make them any form of substantial income. They are too afraid to make the jump.

"When the student is ready the

teacher will appear"
Buddhist Proverb

What did I learn from my friend the wedding planner, and from many people? Sometimes, we look outside ourselves because we cannot see our own strengths and abilities. We go in pursuit of an imagined 'treasure' at the end of the rainbow, when all along were sitting on a real pot of gold.

Transferable skills are not easy to find, it's like counting the hairs on the back of your neck. You either need a mirror or a good friend who can tell you exactly what type of skills you possess.

But here's a way to make this process a lot easier than you think it is.

Start thinking of these definitions:-

Skills Definition - why focus on one skill when you can use them all?

Skills can be:

Abilities that one possesses.

Transferable – skills relevant in any industry. It can also refer to past accomplishments or experiences.

Labour skills – e.g. technical skills, baking, skills in building and DIY projects.

Social skills - Interaction, communication, manners, the ability build relationships with people and connect with them.

Soft skills – Emotional intelligence, IQ, the ability to identify, assess and deal with your emotions in all situations.

Life skills -- Problem solving and managing personal affairs.

Next, fill out this table and begin to observe the pattern in your hobbies and all aspects of life to see if a similar or recurring pattern exists. If there is, you're on the right track to understanding your transferable skills.

Jobs / Careers	Key Skills	Values	Strength	Weakness	Hobbies	Interest	Goals	Outcome
Police	Investigating	Justice	Researching	Admin	Hockey	Human rights	Start a farm	Former Campaigner

Remember, the longer you stay on a job that does not utilise your full capacity and skills, the farther you are from amazing opportunities and the more you become stagnant in that work environment.

"Whenever I'm playing a role that doesn't match my skills, I am taking someone else's job"
Mercy Oruwari

Begin to think of:

What could my purpose be?

- **Purpose** – Your reason for being e.g. helping people change their lifestyle
- **Your Goals** – e.g. Professional and personal: speak, write, teach, travel, transform others
- **Your Objective** – What would you like to achieve? e.g. help more women, and men become confident and truly understand what they were born to do
- **Your Values** – e.g. livelihood, doing things on purpose, being happy, childlike, fun, personal fulfilment
- **Special Niche** – People you really like working with e.g. professionals in their 30s-40s

What is yours?

My purpose is -

_____

_____

My goals are

_____

_____

My objective in life is

to_____

_____

The values that are important to me are

_____

The type of people I would like to work with are
_____ because_____

_____

_____

Then write down what you'd like your <u>mission</u> statement to be, using the questions below:

<u>What do I want?</u>

_____

_____

_____

<u>What do I want people to know me as?</u>

_____

_____

_____

<u>Why are you important? Statement of affirmation - HERE</u>

_____

_____

_____

Mission statement

_____

_____

_____

_____

CLOSING

I want to wish you the very best, as you approach your most crucial decision in your career or current job. Find a place where you call home in the work place. Make a decision that gets you out of your comfort zone and that suits you. Plan a few steps ahead of time. Avoid waiting till it's too late. Live with no regret that you've at least followed your guts and tried.

Whether you choose to quit or embrace your job crisis.

The man in the belly of the whale

A man was given a month to travel to Asia, to bring food and water to people in this small town. The city was full of poverty, debauchery, diseases and hopelessness. Although the man knew he only had 30 days and that this was an emergency, he thought," I have enough time to make a quick stop to another island for a vacation break. Then I'll be on my way."

However his destiny had other plans. When a storm hit the boat, he found himself overboard, swimming for his life and he knew it was his fault. After being violently hit on the head, by a chunk of wood, he felt himself sinking down into a dark abyss. Almost as if he was dragged down by dark invisible forces. He swirled and swirled and swirled into complete darkness. He was, in the belly of a whale. Whilst trapped there for three days and three nights, he began to reflect and wonder how he could somehow turn his life around for the better. If only he could be given another chance, he would go straight to that town in Asia and bring food and water to the people who needed it the most. As that was his calling.

I relate to "The man in the belly of the whale" story because that was my story, of how I procrastinated for 9 years to write this first book, making all sorts of excuses. My 9 years taught me things I should have learnt more quickly. I pray it will never take you 9 years to do what you are supposed to do in life and figure out how to take action for your personal journey.

Dear mum and dad.

Dear Mum and Dad,
I'm sorry it took me so long to write my first book.
I should never have listened to all those people who
constantly discouraged me and those thoughts in my head
that deceived me.
I was a thought-schizophrenic and a Fearaholic.
I made excuses for just about everything, I said money was
an issue when it was not,
I said I needed to pay my bills when I should have just
started working on my dream; I used both of your illnesses
as excuses to hide behind, and felt sorry for myself,
I was hooked on fear like being hooked on crack cocaine.
All these things I said, but they were all a mirage of my
favourite addiction.
Now that I am sober and a recovering Fearaholic,
I promise from now on I will endeavour not to play it
small.
For it is only when I express my unadulterated gift that
others feel empowered to do the same. My purpose gives
other people permission to say 'I can', 'I will' and 'I must'.
If no one is laughing at their gift, then why should they
laugh at mine? I am an artist and I need to express myself
freely.
I'm sad, really sad you won't see this but I know
There's another Mathy in a parallel universe,
A Mathy, whose proud parents have seen her walk in her
purpose
Thank you for being my true inspiration
Hope for someone else who will benefit from this story.
And the wisdom learned. They too shall be inspired.

If you only had 30 days to live, what would you say to your present and future self? Take the time and write a letter to yourself.

_____
_____
_____
_____
_____
_____
_____
_____
_____
_____
_____
_____
_____
_____
_____
_____
_____
_____
_____
_____
_____

"Be an agent of change no matter what you do or where you are in the world"

If you've been inspired by the message in this book, please leave me a little review on amazon.

About Mathy

The first thing you notice when you meet Mathy is her infectious smile and the feeling you've met her before.

Trilingual Mathy grew up in a very multicultural household. By age 3 she was on a plane and lived almost everywhere. From Paris, Belgium, South Africa, Congo, UK, Ireland.

She attended TASOK (The American School of Kinshasa.) In her early days, she was an athlete, vocalist and model. She loves technology, fashion, blogging, cultural events, her nieces and nephews but most of all cupcakes.

Mathy has worked in the careers industry for 14 yrs experience, and has lifelong experience in the creative world. She is a secret artist, coach, author, and lifestyle motivator. Founder of Whathejobisthis blog, helping creative's transition from their 9-5 to their creative calling. Using social media, she has built a business on zero budget.

Other Achievements includes:

Winner of JCI speaking competition and Tedxsquaremile - keynote Speaker at Prospects Graduate's fair- Built a portfolio career using social media a sought after Speaker.

If you are a creative individual in need of coaching, for career transition, boost your confidence or a company who needs a speaker, trainer to engage an audience and boost your client's performance? Then Mathy is the woman for you. Get in touch **whathejobisthis@gmail.com**

www.ingramcontent.com/pod-product-compliance
Lightning Source LLC
Chambersburg PA
CBHW070949180526
45168CB00003B/1178

* 9 7 8 1 5 0 8 5 9 2 1 3 6 *